About Value Tortoise?

Imagine being an investor—someone fascinated by dissecting businesses and financials, delving into macro trends, or running backtests to inform investment decisions.

Now, let's say you decide to explore the world of electric vehicles. You delve into the industry landscape, study the technology, and before you know it, you've spiraled down a rabbit hole, ending up on Google asking, "How does a car work?" After a couple of hours, realizing why engineering wasn't your calling, you take a breather and head to the movies.

But even there, amid overpriced popcorn and a theater barely filled to 20% capacity, your investor's mind kicks in, pondering, "How on earth do they make a profit?" Fast forward to the next day, and you find yourself immersed in research about cars and theaters.

Value Tortoise? It's an investment newsletter that, well, sometimes seems to wander off the investing path. I'm Dhruv Maniyar, the human behind the website, and a former buy-side equity analyst.

Whether I'm dissecting businesses, exploring industry landscapes, or even contemplating the economics of popcorn at the movies, each tangent somehow weaves back into the world of investing. Well, I certainly hope for it to. Because at its core, investing isn't just about crunching numbers or analyzing market trends in isolation. It's about understanding the world around us.

So, if you're looking for an investing newsletter that's not afraid to go off-topic, you should consider subscribing!

Why an investment journal?

Stock prices can swing wildly because of a company's performance, market trends, global events, or even just a tweet from someone influential. When a stock we own shoots up, it's easy to pat ourselves on the back and declare, "I knew that would happen!" But did we really?

Enter the investment journal. Its purpose isn't just to document what we've done but to challenge our thinking. When we jot down our thesis for buying a particular stock—the research, the analysis, the reasons behind our decision—it's like making a commitment to our future selves. We're saying, "Hey, this is why we're doing this, and we want to remember why, even if the stock takes an unexpected turn."

The real magic happens when the stock does move, especially in our favor. Instead of attributing it solely to our genius, we can go back to our journal and see if the actual outcome aligns with what we predicted. It keeps us honest. It's a reality check against hindsight bias, the tricky tendency to see events as predictable or obvious after they've occurred.

And guess what? Sometimes stocks nosedive despite our best research. That's where the journal becomes a teacher. By revisiting our decisions—both the good and the not-so-good—we learn. We improve our investment process.

An investment journal isn't just about the stocks; it's about us—the investor. It's our way of creating a feedback loop, a mechanism to constantly learn and evolve in a world where certainty is a luxury. It's a reminder that successful investing isn't just about making the right moves; it's about understanding why we made them in the first place.

Some useful Mental Models

Here are a few ideas, models, and frameworks that may assist you on your investing journey.

Inversion: Inversion is a thinking tool that flips problem-solving. It focuses on what to avoid rather than what to pursue.

You've heard of Warren Buffett's investing rules, right? "The first rule of investment is, 'Never lose money. The second rule is, never forget Rule 1.'"

His rule isn't about generating excess returns but about avoiding losses—it's about not losing money. It's about inverting the problem.

One of the most significant applications of inversion in investing can be seen in reverse discounted cash flow analysis.

Compounding: Bill Gates once said, "Most people overestimate what they can achieve in a year and underestimate what they can achieve in ten years." This quote touches on our inability to understand exponential growth and our tendency to focus on instant gratification.

In the investing world, we often fail to grasp the power of compounding. It's easy to comprehend the impact of 20% returns for one year, but understanding 20% for 20 straight years is where we often make a mistake.

Feynman Technique: The Feynman technique, named after physicist Richard Feynman, involves simplifying complex concepts to teach them to a child.

Often, in times of uncertainty, we resort to complex language to mask our lack of knowledge. Teaching a concept as if to a child exposes these gaps, revealing areas where our understanding might be lacking.

Luck Vs Skill: Most activities in life involve some amount of luck and skill. Mistaking luck for skill is where the problems begin. Different activities have varying levels of luck involved. A quick way to identify luck's role in an activity is to see if you can purposely lose. For instance:

- A dentist can purposely make mistakes in their job, so it's largely a skilled activity.
- An investor in the short run may find it difficult to purposely lose money, indicating a mix of skill and luck.
- The game "Snakes and Ladders" relies on luck as you cannot purposely lose; it's all on the dice.

It's crucial to consider randomness and avoid jumping to immediate faulty conclusions. You can explore this further in Michael Mauboussin's brilliant book, "The Success Equation."

First Principle Thinking: First-principle thinking involves dissecting complex issues into their fundamental components and devising solutions from scratch. It prioritizes questioning assumptions and understanding core truths.

For instance, in baking a cake, rather than relying on recipes, this approach involves understanding ingredient roles like flour, eggs, sugar, and baking powder. It enables innovative experimentation with ratios and substitutions to create personalized or entirely new types of cakes.

Circle of Competence: The Circle of Competence centers on focusing on what we excel at. But before that, identifying our strengths is key. Mental models like First Principle thinking, Inversion, and the Feynman technique prove invaluable here. Again, let's borrow some wisdom from Warren Buffett. He simplifies his investing approach into three categories:
  1. Yes
  2. No
  3. Too tough

The notion of having a "too tough" category serves to prevent venturing outside one's expertise. While expanding our knowledge over time is desirable, the core idea remains: stay within our area of expertise, ensuring a solid foundation before branching out.

Skin in the game: This mental model might be the simplest yet most crucial on the list. Asking a barber if you need a haircut might not be the wisest move because you're overlooking the barber's incentives. Whenever we seek advice or give instructions, it's vital to consider the incentives of the person providing that guidance.

As Nassim Taleb astutely states, "Don't tell me what you think, tell me what you have in your portfolio."

Illusory Correlation: You may have heard the popular saying, "Correlation does not imply causation". Simply put, just because two things happen together does not mean that one caused the other. I like to split it into four different cases:
  1. X caused Y.
  2. Y caused X.
  3. X and Y did not cause each other. They both may be linked to a third variable like "Z".
  4. Just a random coincidence.

It's worth keeping this in mind before drawing conclusions.

Opportunity cost: Opportunity cost refers to the expense of choosing the next best alternative when making a decision. It essentially revolves around the question, "What am I giving up by choosing this particular option?"

For example, if you spend 3 hours watching a movie, the opportunity cost might include activities like exercising, eating, sleeping or anything that you could have done during that time. In the realm of investing, I believe that the "Cost of Equity" can frequently be seen as an opportunity cost.

Group probability Vs Individual Probability: When 100 people visit a casino for a day, and only 1 person goes broke, the chance of going broke in a single day is set at 1%. However, if someone goes to the casino 100 times, they'll inevitably go broke—it's a 100% chance. The tricky part is, you can't simply use that 1% chance from the group to predict what happens to one person over many visits. There's a significant difference between what happens on average and what happens to one person over time.

Pavlovian Association: The Russian scientist Ivan Pavlov studied the digestive system of dogs. In one experiment, he rang a bell just before giving food to the dog. He repeated this several times until the dog salivated at the sound of the bell alone. The dog's brain started expecting food merely by the sound of the bell, eliminating the need for the presence of food.

Conditioning frequently leads to a specific reaction to a stimulus. For example, during bear markets, we are often primed to anticipate bad news, which can sometimes cause us to overlook obvious signs of better times ahead. This factor contributes to the difficulty of making contrarian bets.

Critical Mass: In nuclear physics, critical mass refers to the smallest amount of fissile material necessary for a sustained nuclear chain reaction. (I really wish I had studied physics better!) When applied in other fields, critical mass often represents the tipping point. Once reached by a firm or product, it profoundly alters the behavior of the system.

Take, for instance, the transition of water from 1 degree to 0 degrees Celsius. Despite being just one degree, the transformation in form is significant. In finance, consider the concept of economies of scale.

Reflexivity: Popularized by George Soros, the theory of reflexivity asserts that investors' decisions aren't solely rooted in reality but rather in their perceptions of reality. These actions, based on their perceptions, influence reality, thus creating a two-way feedback loop where perceptions shape and are shaped by subsequent events.

For example, imagine a scenario where investors collectively believe that the price of a certain commodity will skyrocket due to increasing demand. This belief drives them to buy the commodity, resulting in a surge in its price. As the price continues to rise, their perception of its value strengthens, leading to even more buying and further price escalation. This ongoing cycle of perception influencing action, and action reinforcing perception, vividly illustrates the concept of reflexivity in financial markets.

Inattentional Blindness: In a study by psychologists Daniel Simons and Christopher Chabris, viewers watching a basketball-passing video missed a person in a gorilla suit entering because they were focused on counting passes. This phenomenon, termed inattentional blindness, shows our tendency to overlook obvious things if we don't expect them. In investing, this blindness reminds us of the risk of overlooking the unexpected—a reminder of the need for checklists.

Porter's Five Forces: Porter's five forces is a framework that analyses an industry's competitiveness through five key aspects:
- Threat of new entrants
- Bargaining power of suppliers
- Bargaining power of buyers
- Threat of substitutes
- Intensity of rivalry among competitors.

It helps businesses understand their market's dynamics and competition, shaping strategies to stay competitive and profitable.

Moat Classifications : The term 'Moat' is frequently overused in investing discussions. To bring clarity to this concept, I find Hamilton Helmer's framework particularly valuable. In his insightful book 'Seven Powers,' he outlines seven distinct types of competitive advantages that a company might possess:
- Brand
- Switching Costs
- Scale
- Counter Positioning
- Network Effects
- Cornered Resource
- Process Power

This framework provides a structured approach when contemplating 'Moats' in investing strategies.

Second Order thinking: At some point, while ruling over India, the British were concerned about the ever-increasing Cobra population. To try to reduce it they decided to introduce an incentive. A person would be rewarded for every dead cobra that they brought. This worked wonderfully for a while until the British realized that people had started breeding and killing cobras. When they removed this incentive, people let the Cobras free leading to a further increase in the Cobra population.

Their incentive had created a further problem. As Peter Bevelin writes "Actions have consequences and consequences have further effects". Second and third-order consequences are the ripple effects that occur after an initial action or decision. They represent the indirect outcomes that follow the immediate and visible results. When we make choices or take actions, we often consider the first-order consequences—the direct and immediate results of our decisions. However, it's crucial to delve deeper into the subsequent layers to understand the full impact.

Margin of safety: Margin of safety, as a mental model, embodies the idea of preparing for potential errors or uncertainties in our decisions. It emphasizes acquiring assets or investments at prices well below their intrinsic value.

This deliberate approach acknowledges our fallibility, advocating for a "better safe than sorry" mindset. It encourages a cautious stance, allowing room for misjudgements or unexpected downturns while aiming to safeguard against significant losses.

A research checklist

Wiser individuals have crafted incredible investing checklists. However, if you're seeking a basic template to begin with, this could be a useful starting point.

QUESTIONS WORTH PONDERING
Can you explain how the business runs, to a child?
How was the business founded and how has it evolved over time?
What is the total addressable market? Is it growing?
How much market share does the business currently hold? Is it entering any new markets?
Is the company expected to grow faster than the rest of the market?
Where do you see the business in the next twenty years?
Who is the core customer of the business? Is it diversified or concentrated?
Is the customer very reliant on the business?
Are the products/services a one-time purchase or do they have the possibility of repeat orders?
Is it a very seasonal business?
How is the product/service made?
Are the raw materials used in product manufacturing highly dependent on commodity prices? Have these prices experienced significant volatility? And is the company able to pass on these price fluctuations to customers?
Does the business exhibit a lot of EBITDA margin volatility?
Is the business cyclical in nature?
What type of relation does the business have with its suppliers?
Does the business grow through mergers and acquisitions, or does it grow organically?
Has historical growth been profitable and will it continue?
Is the growth internally funded or is it debt funded? Is the debt in control?
Is it a very Capex heavy business?

How much is the company reinvesting into the business? How has this changed over the years?

What sort of return on investment does the company enjoy? How will it change over time?

Is the company consistently earning above cost of capital?

Does the business enjoy any sustainable competitive advantages?(Moats)

Does the business have the ability to raise prices without losing a lot of customers? What is the pricing power like?

Is the business managed in a centralized or decentralized manner?

Is there room for operating leverage in this business?

How does the level of working capital affect the business's cash flow?

Are there a lot of intangible assets on the balance sheet? How are they amortized?

Do the Net income and Operating cash flow move hand in hand?

Is there a lot of volatility in the depreciation rate?

Do exceptional or one-time expenses constantly show up on the financial statements?

Does the business have any contingent liabilities? Can they be covered easily by the current net income?

How are senior managers compensated?

How did the manager come to lead the business?

Has the promoter shareholding been increasing/decreasing?

Does the management give accurate guidance?

Are you satisfied with the corporate governance of the firm?

Does the stock price display a lot of volatility?

How do the company's valuation multiples, compare to its peers?

Is the current company valuation above or below its historical average? Does it deserve to be where it is?

What growth does the current market value imply? (Reverse DCF)

Does the current price, provide a margin of safety?

A pre-trade checklist

This checklist follows the research checklist. Once you've completed the rigorous groundwork and are ready to execute a trade, why not document your thoughts quantitatively? Wondering how it works? You'll assign a score to each question; the higher the score, the better.

ABOUT THE BUSINESS	SCORE
How well do I understand this business? Can I explain it to a child?	/5
Does the business have a good profit margin?	/5
Is the business ROE/ROC above cost of capital?	/5
Do I expect the ROE/ROC to improve over time?	/5
Do the financials look alright? (Forensic check)	/10
Am I comfortable with the management?	/10
Is the company easily finding good opportunities to reinvest?	/5
Does the company have easy access to capital to grow?	/5
Am I expecting high growth?	/5
Am I expecting profitable growth?	/5
Total Sum	/60

VALUATION & TECHNICAL FACTORS	SCORE
How comfortable am I with the price the company is trading at?	/30
Is the company at a favourable technical point?	/5
Has the promoter ownership been increasing over time?	/5
Total Sum	/40

Summing up both sections provides an aggregate score for the stock out of 100. Remember, this checklist isn't meant to sway your decision but to help record your thoughts in a structured manner.

Consider this a starting point. Customize your checklist—add your questions, scoring system, and more. Make it as detailed or as straightforward as you want. I've integrated pre-trade checklist elements into the journaling section, hopefully making it an easy experience.

Bias Check

We are blessed to be aware of our stupidity. Here's hoping that awareness helps us a bit.

SOME BIASES AND FALLACIES WORTH KNOWING

Anchoring Bias: In financial markets, this bias occurs when investors anchor their investment decisions to a specific price or value. Often the price they paid for a stock. They may hold onto investments waiting for the price to return to the anchor point, regardless of fundamental changes in the market.

Survivorship bias: Survivorship bias occurs when the focus is placed only on the individuals or things that have "survived" a particular process or selection while neglecting those that didn't. For instance, when looking at the performance of investment funds, survivorship bias might occur if only the successful funds that are still active are considered, while the funds that performed poorly and were closed or removed from the market are ignored.

Confirmation bias: It is the tendency to search for, interpret, favor, and recall information that confirms our existing beliefs or hypotheses while disregarding contradictory evidence.

Recency Bias: This bias involves giving more weight to recent events or information while ignoring longer-term trends or historical data. Investors may overly rely on recent market movements without considering broader market cycles.

Sunk Cost Fallacy: Investors sometimes base their decisions on the resources (time, money, effort) already invested rather than on the potential future outcomes. This can lead to holding onto losing investments simply because of the initial investment made.

Hindsight bias: It is the tendency for individuals to perceive past events as having been more predictable than they actually were before they happened. In investing, it can create false confidence and distort decision-making based on past events that seem clearer in hindsight than they actually were.

Bandwagon Fallacy: It occurs when someone argues that a statement must be true because it's popular or because a lot of people believe it. However, popularity or widespread belief doesn't necessarily make an idea true or valid —it's the evidence and reasoning behind it that matters.

Self Serving Bias: In the context of financial markets, this bias leads investors to attribute their successful investment choices to their skill while attributing losses to external factors like market volatility or unforeseeable events.

Pre Trade Thoughts

Stock _______________________   Date _______________________

Price _______________________   Quantity _______________________

THOUGHTS BEFORE BUYING	INPUTS
How confident are you in the business model?	😣😖😐🙂😃
How confident are you in the management?	😣😖😐🙂😃
Rank the financial strength of the firm	😣😖😐🙂😃
How comfortable are you with the valuation of the firm?	😣😖😐🙂😃
Within what price range would you feel comfortable adding this stock?	
What's the maximum percentage of your portfolio you're comfortable investing in this stock?	

What am I expecting? (Circle all that apply)

Falling interest rates	Reduction in debt	Clearly undervalued
Positive capex cycle	Change in business model	Consistent compounder
Demand-supply mismatch	Merger or Acquisition	Dividend play
Positive government policies	Positive management change	Recession resistant play
Sector Tailwind/Seasonal	Accelerated growth	20+ Year Growth Story
Turnaround story	Enhanced product offerings	Technical signal
Inflation Hedge	Improving Financials	Momentum Play

In 2 lines explain why you are buying this stock

Post Trade Thoughts

Stock _______________________   Date _______________________

Price _______________________   Quantity _______________________

THOUGHTS AFTER SELLING	INPUTS
How confident are you in the business model?	😠😟😐🙂😃
How confident are you in the management?	😠😟😐🙂😃
Rank the financial strength of the firm	😠😟😐🙂😃
How comfortable are you with the valuation of the firm?	😠😟😐🙂😃
If you're selling gradually over time, what price range feels comfortable for you to sell the stock within?	
What return have you generated through this investment?	

Why did I sell the stock?

Did the investment thesis play out as planned?

Pre Trade Thoughts

Stock ....   Date ....

Price ....   Quantity ....

THOUGHTS BEFORE BUYING	INPUTS
How confident are you in the business model?	😟😟😐😊😀
How confident are you in the management?	😟😟😐😊😀
Rank the financial strength of the firm	😟😟😐😊😀
How comfortable are you with the valuation of the firm?	😟😟😐😊😀
Within what price range would you feel comfortable adding this stock?	
What's the maximum percentage of your portfolio you're comfortable investing in this stock?	

What am I expecting? (Circle all that apply)

Falling interest rates	Reduction in debt	Clearly undervalued
Positive capex cycle	Change in business model	Consistent compounder
Demand-supply mismatch	Merger or Acquisition	Dividend play
Positive government policies	Positive management change	Recession resistant play
Sector Tailwind/Seasonal	Accelerated growth	20+ Year Growth Story
Turnaround story	Enhanced product offerings	Technical signal
Inflation Hedge	Improving Financials	Momentum Play

In 2 lines explain why you are buying this stock

Post Trade Thoughts

Stock ....   Date ....

Price ....   Quantity ....

THOUGHTS AFTER SELLING	INPUTS
How confident are you in the business model?	😠😦😐😊😀
How confident are you in the management?	😠😦😐😊😀
Rank the financial strength of the firm	😠😦😐😊😀
How comfortable are you with the valuation of the firm?	😠😦😐😊😀
If you're selling gradually over time, what price range feels comfortable for you to sell the stock within?	
What return have you generated through this investment?	

Why did I sell the stock?

Did the investment thesis play out as planned?

Pre Trade Thoughts

Stock ....   Date ....

Price ....   Quantity ....

THOUGHTS BEFORE BUYING	INPUTS
How confident are you in the business model?	😖😟😐🙂😄
How confident are you in the management?	😖😟😐🙂😄
Rank the financial strength of the firm	😖😟😐🙂😄
How comfortable are you with the valuation of the firm?	😖😟😐🙂😄
Within what price range would you feel comfortable adding this stock?	
What's the maximum percentage of your portfolio you're comfortable investing in this stock?	

What am I expecting? (Circle all that apply)

Falling interest rates	Reduction in debt	Clearly undervalued
Positive capex cycle	Change in business model	Consistent compounder
Demand-supply mismatch	Merger or Acquisition	Dividend play
Positive government policies	Positive management change	Recession resistant play
Sector Tailwind/Seasonal	Accelerated growth	20+ Year Growth Story
Turnaround story	Enhanced product offerings	Technical signal
Inflation Hedge	Improving Financials	Momentum Play

In 2 lines explain why you are buying this stock

Post Trade Thoughts

Stock ....   Date ....

Price ....   Quantity ....

THOUGHTS AFTER SELLING	INPUTS
How confident are you in the business model?	😩😟😐🙂😀
How confident are you in the management?	😩😟😐🙂😀
Rank the financial strength of the firm	😩😟😐🙂😀
How comfortable are you with the valuation of the firm?	😩😟😐🙂😀
If you're selling gradually over time, what price range feels comfortable for you to sell the stock within?	
What return have you generated through this investment?	

Why did I sell the stock?

Did the investment thesis play out as planned?

Pre Trade Thoughts

Stock _______________________________   Date _______________________________

Price _______________________________   Quantity _______________________________

THOUGHTS BEFORE BUYING	INPUTS
How confident are you in the business model?	😣😟😐😊😃
How confident are you in the management?	😣😟😐😊😃
Rank the financial strength of the firm	😣😟😐😊😃
How comfortable are you with the valuation of the firm?	😣😟😐😊😃
Within what price range would you feel comfortable adding this stock?	
What's the maximum percentage of your portfolio you're comfortable investing in this stock?	

What am I expecting? (Circle all that apply)

Falling interest rates	Reduction in debt	Clearly undervalued
Positive capex cycle	Change in business model	Consistent compounder
Demand-supply mismatch	Merger or Acquisition	Dividend play
Positive government policies	Positive management change	Recession resistant play
Sector Tailwind/Seasonal	Accelerated growth	20+ Year Growth Story
Turnaround story	Enhanced product offerings	Technical signal
Inflation Hedge	Improving Financials	Momentum Play

In 2 lines explain why you are buying this stock

Post Trade Thoughts

Stock __________________________   Date __________________________

Price __________________________   Quantity __________________________

THOUGHTS AFTER SELLING	INPUTS
How confident are you in the business model?	😣😟😐😊😄
How confident are you in the management?	😣😟😐😊😄
Rank the financial strength of the firm	😣😟😐😊😄
How comfortable are you with the valuation of the firm?	😣😟😐😊😄
If you're selling gradually over time, what price range feels comfortable for you to sell the stock within?	
What return have you generated through this investment?	

Why did I sell the stock?

Did the investment thesis play out as planned?

Pre Trade Thoughts

Stock ....   Date ....

Price ....   Quantity ....

THOUGHTS BEFORE BUYING	INPUTS
How confident are you in the business model?	😞😟😐🙂😀
How confident are you in the management?	😞😟😐🙂😀
Rank the financial strength of the firm	😞😟😐🙂😀
How comfortable are you with the valuation of the firm?	😞😟😐🙂😀
Within what price range would you feel comfortable adding this stock?	
What's the maximum percentage of your portfolio you're comfortable investing in this stock?	

What am I expecting? (Circle all that apply)

Falling interest rates	Reduction in debt	Clearly undervalued
Positive capex cycle	Change in business model	Consistent compounder
Demand-supply mismatch	Merger or Acquisition	Dividend play
Positive government policies	Positive management change	Recession resistant play
Sector Tailwind/Seasonal	Accelerated growth	20+ Year Growth Story
Turnaround story	Enhanced product offerings	Technical signal
Inflation Hedge	Improving Financials	Momentum Play

In 2 lines explain why you are buying this stock

Post Trade Thoughts

Stock ....   Date ....

Price ....   Quantity ....

THOUGHTS AFTER SELLING	INPUTS
How confident are you in the business model?	😟😦😐😊😃
How confident are you in the management?	😟😦😐😊😃
Rank the financial strength of the firm	😟😦😐😊😃
How comfortable are you with the valuation of the firm?	😟😦😐😊😃
If you're selling gradually over time, what price range feels comfortable for you to sell the stock within?	
What return have you generated through this investment?	

Why did I sell the stock?

Did the investment thesis play out as planned?

Pre Trade Thoughts

Stock _______________________   Date _______________________

Price _______________________   Quantity _______________________

THOUGHTS BEFORE BUYING	INPUTS
How confident are you in the business model?	😠 😧 😐 🙂 😀
How confident are you in the management?	😠 😧 😐 🙂 😀
Rank the financial strength of the firm	😠 😧 😐 🙂 😀
How comfortable are you with the valuation of the firm?	😠 😧 😐 🙂 😀
Within what price range would you feel comfortable adding this stock?	
What's the maximum percentage of your portfolio you're comfortable investing in this stock?	

What am I expecting? (Circle all that apply)

Falling interest rates	Reduction in debt	Clearly undervalued
Positive capex cycle	Change in business model	Consistent compounder
Demand-supply mismatch	Merger or Acquisition	Dividend play
Positive government policies	Positive management change	Recession resistant play
Sector Tailwind/Seasonal	Accelerated growth	20+ Year Growth Story
Turnaround story	Enhanced product offerings	Technical signal
Inflation Hedge	Improving Financials	Momentum Play

In 2 lines explain why you are buying this stock

Post Trade Thoughts

Stock ....   Date ....

Price ....   Quantity ....

THOUGHTS AFTER SELLING	INPUTS
How confident are you in the business model?	😣😟😐🙂😀
How confident are you in the management?	😣😟😐🙂😀
Rank the financial strength of the firm	😣😟😐🙂😀
How comfortable are you with the valuation of the firm?	😣😟😐🙂😀
If you're selling gradually over time, what price range feels comfortable for you to sell the stock within?	
What return have you generated through this investment?	

Why did I sell the stock?

Did the investment thesis play out as planned?

Pre Trade Thoughts

Stock ....   Date ....

Price ....   Quantity ....

THOUGHTS BEFORE BUYING	INPUTS
How confident are you in the business model?	😠😟😐🙂😄
How confident are you in the management?	😠😟😐🙂😄
Rank the financial strength of the firm	😠😟😐🙂😄
How comfortable are you with the valuation of the firm?	😠😟😐🙂😄
Within what price range would you feel comfortable adding this stock?	
What's the maximum percentage of your portfolio you're comfortable investing in this stock?	

What am I expecting? (Circle all that apply)

Falling interest rates	Reduction in debt	Clearly undervalued
Positive capex cycle	Change in business model	Consistent compounder
Demand-supply mismatch	Merger or Acquisition	Dividend play
Positive government policies	Positive management change	Recession resistant play
Sector Tailwind/Seasonal	Accelerated growth	20+ Year Growth Story
Turnaround story	Enhanced product offerings	Technical signal
Inflation Hedge	Improving Financials	Momentum Play

In 2 lines explain why you are buying this stock

Post Trade Thoughts

Stock ....   Date ....

Price ....   Quantity ....

THOUGHTS AFTER SELLING	INPUTS
How confident are you in the business model?	☹☹😐🙂😀
How confident are you in the management?	☹☹😐🙂😀
Rank the financial strength of the firm	☹☹😐🙂😀
How comfortable are you with the valuation of the firm?	☹☹😐🙂😀
If you're selling gradually over time, what price range feels comfortable for you to sell the stock within?	
What return have you generated through this investment?	

Why did I sell the stock?

Did the investment thesis play out as planned?

Pre Trade Thoughts

Stock ....   Date ....

Price ....   Quantity ....

THOUGHTS BEFORE BUYING	INPUTS
How confident are you in the business model?	😞😟😐🙂😀
How confident are you in the management?	😞😟😐🙂😀
Rank the financial strength of the firm	😞😟😐🙂😀
How comfortable are you with the valuation of the firm?	😞😟😐🙂😀
Within what price range would you feel comfortable adding this stock?	
What's the maximum percentage of your portfolio you're comfortable investing in this stock?	

What am I expecting? (Circle all that apply)

Falling interest rates	Reduction in debt	Clearly undervalued
Positive capex cycle	Change in business model	Consistent compounder
Demand-supply mismatch	Merger or Acquisition	Dividend play
Positive government policies	Positive management change	Recession resistant play
Sector Tailwind/Seasonal	Accelerated growth	20+ Year Growth Story
Turnaround story	Enhanced product offerings	Technical signal
Inflation Hedge	Improving Financials	Momentum Play

In 2 lines explain why you are buying this stock

Post Trade Thoughts

Stock ....   Date ....

Price ....   Quantity ....

THOUGHTS AFTER SELLING	INPUTS
How confident are you in the business model?	😟😕😐🙂😀
How confident are you in the management?	😟😕😐🙂😀
Rank the financial strength of the firm	😟😕😐🙂😀
How comfortable are you with the valuation of the firm?	😟😕😐🙂😀
If you're selling gradually over time, what price range feels comfortable for you to sell the stock within?	
What return have you generated through this investment?	

Why did I sell the stock?

Did the investment thesis play out as planned?

Pre Trade Thoughts

Stock _______________________   Date _______________________

Price _______________________   Quantity _______________________

THOUGHTS BEFORE BUYING	INPUTS
How confident are you in the business model?	😠😩😐😊😃
How confident are you in the management?	😠😩😐😊😃
Rank the financial strength of the firm	😠😩😐😊😃
How comfortable are you with the valuation of the firm?	😠😩😐😊😃
Within what price range would you feel comfortable adding this stock?	
What's the maximum percentage of your portfolio you're comfortable investing in this stock?	

What am I expecting? (Circle all that apply)

Falling interest rates	Reduction in debt	Clearly undervalued
Positive capex cycle	Change in business model	Consistent compounder
Demand-supply mismatch	Merger or Acquisition	Dividend play
Positive government policies	Positive management change	Recession resistant play
Sector Tailwind/Seasonal	Accelerated growth	20+ Year Growth Story
Turnaround story	Enhanced product offerings	Technical signal
Inflation Hedge	Improving Financials	Momentum Play

In 2 lines explain why you are buying this stock

Post Trade Thoughts

Stock ....   Date ....

Price ....   Quantity ....

THOUGHTS AFTER SELLING	INPUTS
How confident are you in the business model?	☹☹☺☺☺
How confident are you in the management?	☹☹☺☺☺
Rank the financial strength of the firm	☹☹☺☺☺
How comfortable are you with the valuation of the firm?	☹☹☺☺☺
If you're selling gradually over time, what price range feels comfortable for you to sell the stock within?	
What return have you generated through this investment?	

Why did I sell the stock?

Did the investment thesis play out as planned?

Pre Trade Thoughts

Stock ____________________________   Date ____________________

Price ____________________________   Quantity ________________

THOUGHTS BEFORE BUYING	INPUTS
How confident are you in the business model?	😞😟😐🙂😀
How confident are you in the management?	😞😟😐🙂😀
Rank the financial strength of the firm	😞😟😐🙂😀
How comfortable are you with the valuation of the firm?	😞😟😐🙂😀
Within what price range would you feel comfortable adding this stock?	
What's the maximum percentage of your portfolio you're comfortable investing in this stock?	

What am I expecting? (Circle all that apply)

Falling interest rates	Reduction in debt	Clearly undervalued
Positive capex cycle	Change in business model	Consistent compounder
Demand-supply mismatch	Merger or Acquisition	Dividend play
Positive government policies	Positive management change	Recession resistant play
Sector Tailwind/Seasonal	Accelerated growth	20+ Year Growth Story
Turnaround story	Enhanced product offerings	Technical signal
Inflation Hedge	Improving Financials	Momentum Play

In 2 lines explain why you are buying this stock

Post Trade Thoughts

Stock _______________________   Date _______________________

Price _______________________   Quantity _______________________

THOUGHTS AFTER SELLING	INPUTS
How confident are you in the business model?	😣😢😐😊😃
How confident are you in the management?	😣😢😐😊😃
Rank the financial strength of the firm	😣😢😐😊😃
How comfortable are you with the valuation of the firm?	😣😢😐😊😃
If you're selling gradually over time, what price range feels comfortable for you to sell the stock within?	
What return have you generated through this investment?	

Why did I sell the stock?

Did the investment thesis play out as planned?

Pre Trade Thoughts

Stock _______________________   Date _______________________

Price _______________________   Quantity _______________________

THOUGHTS BEFORE BUYING	INPUTS
How confident are you in the business model?	😟😣😐😊😃
How confident are you in the management?	😟😣😐😊😃
Rank the financial strength of the firm	😟😣😐😊😃
How comfortable are you with the valuation of the firm?	😟😣😐😊😃
Within what price range would you feel comfortable adding this stock?	
What's the maximum percentage of your portfolio you're comfortable investing in this stock?	

What am I expecting? (Circle all that apply)

Falling interest rates	Reduction in debt	Clearly undervalued
Positive capex cycle	Change in business model	Consistent compounder
Demand-supply mismatch	Merger or Acquisition	Dividend play
Positive government policies	Positive management change	Recession resistant play
Sector Tailwind/Seasonal	Accelerated growth	20+ Year Growth Story
Turnaround story	Enhanced product offerings	Technical signal
Inflation Hedge	Improving Financials	Momentum Play

In 2 lines explain why you are buying this stock

Post Trade Thoughts

Stock _______________________   Date _______________________

Price _______________________   Quantity _______________________

THOUGHTS AFTER SELLING	INPUTS
How confident are you in the business model?	😠😦😐😊😃
How confident are you in the management?	😠😦😐😊😃
Rank the financial strength of the firm	😠😦😐😊😃
How comfortable are you with the valuation of the firm?	😠😦😐😊😃
If you're selling gradually over time, what price range feels comfortable for you to sell the stock within?	
What return have you generated through this investment?	

Why did I sell the stock?

Did the investment thesis play out as planned?

Pre Trade Thoughts

Stock ....   Date ....

Price ....   Quantity ....

THOUGHTS BEFORE BUYING	INPUTS
How confident are you in the business model?	☹ ☹ 😐 🙂 😀
How confident are you in the management?	☹ ☹ 😐 🙂 😀
Rank the financial strength of the firm	☹ ☹ 😐 🙂 😀
How comfortable are you with the valuation of the firm?	☹ ☹ 😐 🙂 😀
Within what price range would you feel comfortable adding this stock?	
What's the maximum percentage of your portfolio you're comfortable investing in this stock?	

What am I expecting? (Circle all that apply)

Falling interest rates	Reduction in debt	Clearly undervalued
Positive capex cycle	Change in business model	Consistent compounder
Demand-supply mismatch	Merger or Acquisition	Dividend play
Positive government policies	Positive management change	Recession resistant play
Sector Tailwind/Seasonal	Accelerated growth	20+ Year Growth Story
Turnaround story	Enhanced product offerings	Technical signal
Inflation Hedge	Improving Financials	Momentum Play

In 2 lines explain why you are buying this stock

Post Trade Thoughts

Stock ....

Date ....

Price ....

Quantity ....

THOUGHTS AFTER SELLING	INPUTS
How confident are you in the business model?	☹☹😐😊😄
How confident are you in the management?	☹☹😐😊😄
Rank the financial strength of the firm	☹☹😐😊😄
How comfortable are you with the valuation of the firm?	☹☹😐😊😄
If you're selling gradually over time, what price range feels comfortable for you to sell the stock within?	
What return have you generated through this investment?	

Why did I sell the stock?

Did the investment thesis play out as planned?

Pre Trade Thoughts

Stock ___________________________   Date ___________________

Price ___________________________   Quantity _______________

THOUGHTS BEFORE BUYING	INPUTS
How confident are you in the business model?	☹☹😐😊😄
How confident are you in the management?	☹☹😐😊😄
Rank the financial strength of the firm	☹☹😐😊😄
How comfortable are you with the valuation of the firm?	☹☹😐😊😄
Within what price range would you feel comfortable adding this stock?	
What's the maximum percentage of your portfolio you're comfortable investing in this stock?	

What am I expecting? (Circle all that apply)

Falling interest rates	Reduction in debt	Clearly undervalued
Positive capex cycle	Change in business model	Consistent compounder
Demand-supply mismatch	Merger or Acquisition	Dividend play
Positive government policies	Positive management change	Recession resistant play
Sector Tailwind/Seasonal	Accelerated growth	20+ Year Growth Story
Turnaround story	Enhanced product offerings	Technical signal
Inflation Hedge	Improving Financials	Momentum Play

In 2 lines explain why you are buying this stock

Post Trade Thoughts

Stock ....   Date ....

Price ....   Quantity ....

THOUGHTS AFTER SELLING	INPUTS
How confident are you in the business model?	😫😟😐🙂😀
How confident are you in the management?	😫😟😐🙂😀
Rank the financial strength of the firm	😫😟😐🙂😀
How comfortable are you with the valuation of the firm?	😫😟😐🙂😀
If you're selling gradually over time, what price range feels comfortable for you to sell the stock within?	
What return have you generated through this investment?	

Why did I sell the stock?

Did the investment thesis play out as planned?

Pre Trade Thoughts

Stock .... Date ....

Price .... Quantity ....

THOUGHTS BEFORE BUYING	INPUTS
How confident are you in the business model?	☹ ☹ 😐 🙂 😀
How confident are you in the management?	☹ ☹ 😐 🙂 😀
Rank the financial strength of the firm	☹ ☹ 😐 🙂 😀
How comfortable are you with the valuation of the firm?	☹ ☹ 😐 🙂 😀
Within what price range would you feel comfortable adding this stock?	
What's the maximum percentage of your portfolio you're comfortable investing in this stock?	

What am I expecting? (Circle all that apply)

Falling interest rates	Reduction in debt	Clearly undervalued
Positive capex cycle	Change in business model	Consistent compounder
Demand-supply mismatch	Merger or Acquisition	Dividend play
Positive government policies	Positive management change	Recession resistant play
Sector Tailwind/Seasonal	Accelerated growth	20+ Year Growth Story
Turnaround story	Enhanced product offerings	Technical signal
Inflation Hedge	Improving Financials	Momentum Play

In 2 lines explain why you are buying this stock

Post Trade Thoughts

Stock ______________________   Date ______________________

Price ______________________   Quantity ______________________

THOUGHTS AFTER SELLING	INPUTS
How confident are you in the business model?	😣 😟 😐 😊 😀
How confident are you in the management?	😣 😟 😐 😊 😀
Rank the financial strength of the firm	😣 😟 😐 😊 😀
How comfortable are you with the valuation of the firm?	😣 😟 😐 😊 😀
If you're selling gradually over time, what price range feels comfortable for you to sell the stock within?	
What return have you generated through this investment?	

Why did I sell the stock?

Did the investment thesis play out as planned?

Pre Trade Thoughts

Stock ______________________________   Date ______________________________

Price ______________________________   Quantity ______________________________

THOUGHTS BEFORE BUYING	INPUTS
How confident are you in the business model?	😫😟😐🙂😀
How confident are you in the management?	😫😟😐🙂😀
Rank the financial strength of the firm	😫😟😐🙂😀
How comfortable are you with the valuation of the firm?	😫😟😐🙂😀
Within what price range would you feel comfortable adding this stock?	
What's the maximum percentage of your portfolio you're comfortable investing in this stock?	

What am I expecting? (Circle all that apply)

Falling interest rates	Reduction in debt	Clearly undervalued
Positive capex cycle	Change in business model	Consistent compounder
Demand-supply mismatch	Merger or Acquisition	Dividend play
Positive government policies	Positive management change	Recession resistant play
Sector Tailwind/Seasonal	Accelerated growth	20+ Year Growth Story
Turnaround story	Enhanced product offerings	Technical signal
Inflation Hedge	Improving Financials	Momentum Play

In 2 lines explain why you are buying this stock

Post Trade Thoughts

Stock ....   Date ....

Price ....   Quantity ....

THOUGHTS AFTER SELLING	INPUTS
How confident are you in the business model?	😣 😖 😐 😊 😁
How confident are you in the management?	😣 😖 😐 😊 😁
Rank the financial strength of the firm	😣 😖 😐 😊 😁
How comfortable are you with the valuation of the firm?	😣 😖 😐 😊 😁
If you're selling gradually over time, what price range feels comfortable for you to sell the stock within?	
What return have you generated through this investment?	

Why did I sell the stock?

Did the investment thesis play out as planned?

Pre Trade Thoughts

Stock .... Date ....

Price .... Quantity ....

THOUGHTS BEFORE BUYING	INPUTS
How confident are you in the business model?	😧😦😐🙂😀
How confident are you in the management?	😧😦😐🙂😀
Rank the financial strength of the firm	😧😦😐🙂😀
How comfortable are you with the valuation of the firm?	😧😦😐🙂😀
Within what price range would you feel comfortable adding this stock?	
What's the maximum percentage of your portfolio you're comfortable investing in this stock?	

What am I expecting? (Circle all that apply)

Falling interest rates	Reduction in debt	Clearly undervalued
Positive capex cycle	Change in business model	Consistent compounder
Demand-supply mismatch	Merger or Acquisition	Dividend play
Positive government policies	Positive management change	Recession resistant play
Sector Tailwind/Seasonal	Accelerated growth	20+ Year Growth Story
Turnaround story	Enhanced product offerings	Technical signal
Inflation Hedge	Improving Financials	Momentum Play

In 2 lines explain why you are buying this stock

Post Trade Thoughts

Stock _____________________________   Date _____________________________

Price _____________________________   Quantity _____________________________

THOUGHTS AFTER SELLING	INPUTS
How confident are you in the business model?	😣 😟 😐 🙂 😀
How confident are you in the management?	😣 😟 😐 🙂 😀
Rank the financial strength of the firm	😣 😟 😐 🙂 😀
How comfortable are you with the valuation of the firm?	😣 😟 😐 🙂 😀
If you're selling gradually over time, what price range feels comfortable for you to sell the stock within?	
What return have you generated through this investment?	

Why did I sell the stock?

Did the investment thesis play out as planned?

Pre Trade Thoughts

Stock ....

Date ....

Price ....

Quantity ....

THOUGHTS BEFORE BUYING	INPUTS
How confident are you in the business model?	😦😩😐😊😃
How confident are you in the management?	😦😩😐😊😃
Rank the financial strength of the firm	😦😩😐😊😃
How comfortable are you with the valuation of the firm?	😦😩😐😊😃
Within what price range would you feel comfortable adding this stock?	
What's the maximum percentage of your portfolio you're comfortable investing in this stock?	

What am I expecting? (Circle all that apply)

Falling interest rates	Reduction in debt	Clearly undervalued
Positive capex cycle	Change in business model	Consistent compounder
Demand-supply mismatch	Merger or Acquisition	Dividend play
Positive government policies	Positive management change	Recession resistant play
Sector Tailwind/Seasonal	Accelerated growth	20+ Year Growth Story
Turnaround story	Enhanced product offerings	Technical signal
Inflation Hedge	Improving Financials	Momentum Play

In 2 lines explain why you are buying this stock

Post Trade Thoughts

Stock _______________________   Date _______________________

Price _______________________   Quantity _______________________

THOUGHTS AFTER SELLING	INPUTS
How confident are you in the business model?	☹ ☹ 😐 😊 😀
How confident are you in the management?	☹ ☹ 😐 😊 😀
Rank the financial strength of the firm	☹ ☹ 😐 😊 😀
How comfortable are you with the valuation of the firm?	☹ ☹ 😐 😊 😀
If you're selling gradually over time, what price range feels comfortable for you to sell the stock within?	
What return have you generated through this investment?	

Why did I sell the stock?

Did the investment thesis play out as planned?

Pre Trade Thoughts

Stock ....   Date ....

Price ....   Quantity ....

THOUGHTS BEFORE BUYING	INPUTS
How confident are you in the business model?	😟😦😐🙂😀
How confident are you in the management?	😟😦😐🙂😀
Rank the financial strength of the firm	😟😦😐🙂😀
How comfortable are you with the valuation of the firm?	😟😦😐🙂😀
Within what price range would you feel comfortable adding this stock?	
What's the maximum percentage of your portfolio you're comfortable investing in this stock?	

What am I expecting? (Circle all that apply)

Falling interest rates	Reduction in debt	Clearly undervalued
Positive capex cycle	Change in business model	Consistent compounder
Demand-supply mismatch	Merger or Acquisition	Dividend play
Positive government policies	Positive management change	Recession resistant play
Sector Tailwind/Seasonal	Accelerated growth	20+ Year Growth Story
Turnaround story	Enhanced product offerings	Technical signal
Inflation Hedge	Improving Financials	Momentum Play

In 2 lines explain why you are buying this stock

Post Trade Thoughts

Stock ___________________________   Date ___________________________

Price ___________________________   Quantity ___________________________

THOUGHTS AFTER SELLING	INPUTS
How confident are you in the business model?	😣😖😐😊😃
How confident are you in the management?	😣😖😐😊😃
Rank the financial strength of the firm	😣😖😐😊😃
How comfortable are you with the valuation of the firm?	😣😖😐😊😃
If you're selling gradually over time, what price range feels comfortable for you to sell the stock within?	
What return have you generated through this investment?	

Why did I sell the stock?

Did the investment thesis play out as planned?

Pre Trade Thoughts

Stock .... Date ....

Price .... Quantity ....

THOUGHTS BEFORE BUYING	INPUTS
How confident are you in the business model?	😟😟😐😊😁
How confident are you in the management?	😟😟😐😊😁
Rank the financial strength of the firm	😟😟😐😊😁
How comfortable are you with the valuation of the firm?	😟😟😐😊😁
Within what price range would you feel comfortable adding this stock?	
What's the maximum percentage of your portfolio you're comfortable investing in this stock?	

What am I expecting? (Circle all that apply)

Falling interest rates	Reduction in debt	Clearly undervalued
Positive capex cycle	Change in business model	Consistent compounder
Demand-supply mismatch	Merger or Acquisition	Dividend play
Positive government policies	Positive management change	Recession resistant play
Sector Tailwind/Seasonal	Accelerated growth	20+ Year Growth Story
Turnaround story	Enhanced product offerings	Technical signal
Inflation Hedge	Improving Financials	Momentum Play

In 2 lines explain why you are buying this stock

Post Trade Thoughts

Stock ___________________________   Date ___________________________

Price ___________________________   Quantity ___________________________

THOUGHTS AFTER SELLING	INPUTS
How confident are you in the business model?	😣 😟 😐 🙂 😀
How confident are you in the management?	😣 😟 😐 🙂 😀
Rank the financial strength of the firm	😣 😟 😐 🙂 😀
How comfortable are you with the valuation of the firm?	😣 😟 😐 🙂 😀
If you're selling gradually over time, what price range feels comfortable for you to sell the stock within?	
What return have you generated through this investment?	

Why did I sell the stock?

Did the investment thesis play out as planned?

Pre Trade Thoughts

Stock .... Date ....

Price .... Quantity ....

THOUGHTS BEFORE BUYING	INPUTS
How confident are you in the business model?	☹️☹️😐😊😀
How confident are you in the management?	☹️☹️😐😊😀
Rank the financial strength of the firm	☹️☹️😐😊😀
How comfortable are you with the valuation of the firm?	☹️☹️😐😊😀
Within what price range would you feel comfortable adding this stock?	
What's the maximum percentage of your portfolio you're comfortable investing in this stock?	

What am I expecting? (Circle all that apply)

Falling interest rates	Reduction in debt	Clearly undervalued
Positive capex cycle	Change in business model	Consistent compounder
Demand-supply mismatch	Merger or Acquisition	Dividend play
Positive government policies	Positive management change	Recession resistant play
Sector Tailwind/Seasonal	Accelerated growth	20+ Year Growth Story
Turnaround story	Enhanced product offerings	Technical signal
Inflation Hedge	Improving Financials	Momentum Play

In 2 lines explain why you are buying this stock

Post Trade Thoughts

Stock ....   Date ....

Price ....   Quantity ....

THOUGHTS AFTER SELLING	INPUTS
How confident are you in the business model?	😖😦😐😊😄
How confident are you in the management?	😖😦😐😊😄
Rank the financial strength of the firm	😖😦😐😊😄
How comfortable are you with the valuation of the firm?	😖😦😐😊😄
If you're selling gradually over time, what price range feels comfortable for you to sell the stock within?	
What return have you generated through this investment?	

Why did I sell the stock?

Did the investment thesis play out as planned?

Pre Trade Thoughts

Stock _______________________   Date _______________________

Price _______________________   Quantity _______________________

THOUGHTS BEFORE BUYING	INPUTS
How confident are you in the business model?	😣😩😐🙂😄
How confident are you in the management?	😣😩😐🙂😄
Rank the financial strength of the firm	😣😩😐🙂😄
How comfortable are you with the valuation of the firm?	😣😩😐🙂😄
Within what price range would you feel comfortable adding this stock?	
What's the maximum percentage of your portfolio you're comfortable investing in this stock?	

What am I expecting? (Circle all that apply)

Falling interest rates	Reduction in debt	Clearly undervalued
Positive capex cycle	Change in business model	Consistent compounder
Demand-supply mismatch	Merger or Acquisition	Dividend play
Positive government policies	Positive management change	Recession resistant play
Sector Tailwind/Seasonal	Accelerated growth	20+ Year Growth Story
Turnaround story	Enhanced product offerings	Technical signal
Inflation Hedge	Improving Financials	Momentum Play

In 2 lines explain why you are buying this stock

Post Trade Thoughts

Stock .... Date ....

Price .... Quantity ....

THOUGHTS AFTER SELLING	INPUTS
How confident are you in the business model?	😣😖😐😊😃
How confident are you in the management?	😣😖😐😊😃
Rank the financial strength of the firm	😣😖😐😊😃
How comfortable are you with the valuation of the firm?	😣😖😐😊😃
If you're selling gradually over time, what price range feels comfortable for you to sell the stock within?	
What return have you generated through this investment?	

Why did I sell the stock?

Did the investment thesis play out as planned?

Pre Trade Thoughts

Stock ....   Date ....

Price ....   Quantity ....

THOUGHTS BEFORE BUYING	INPUTS
How confident are you in the business model?	☹ ☹ 😐 🙂 😃
How confident are you in the management?	☹ ☹ 😐 🙂 😃
Rank the financial strength of the firm	☹ ☹ 😐 🙂 😃
How comfortable are you with the valuation of the firm?	☹ ☹ 😐 🙂 😃
Within what price range would you feel comfortable adding this stock?	
What's the maximum percentage of your portfolio you're comfortable investing in this stock?	

What am I expecting? (Circle all that apply)

Falling interest rates	Reduction in debt	Clearly undervalued
Positive capex cycle	Change in business model	Consistent compounder
Demand-supply mismatch	Merger or Acquisition	Dividend play
Positive government policies	Positive management change	Recession resistant play
Sector Tailwind/Seasonal	Accelerated growth	20+ Year Growth Story
Turnaround story	Enhanced product offerings	Technical signal
Inflation Hedge	Improving Financials	Momentum Play

In 2 lines explain why you are buying this stock

Post Trade Thoughts

Stock _______________________   Date _______________________

Price _______________________   Quantity _______________________

THOUGHTS AFTER SELLING	INPUTS
How confident are you in the business model?	☹ ☹ 😐 🙂 😀
How confident are you in the management?	☹ ☹ 😐 🙂 😀
Rank the financial strength of the firm	☹ ☹ 😐 🙂 😀
How comfortable are you with the valuation of the firm?	☹ ☹ 😐 🙂 😀
If you're selling gradually over time, what price range feels comfortable for you to sell the stock within?	
What return have you generated through this investment?	

Why did I sell the stock?

Did the investment thesis play out as planned?

Pre Trade Thoughts

Stock ....   Date ....

Price ....   Quantity ....

THOUGHTS BEFORE BUYING	INPUTS
How confident are you in the business model?	😣😖😐🙂😄
How confident are you in the management?	😣😖😐🙂😄
Rank the financial strength of the firm	😣😖😐🙂😄
How comfortable are you with the valuation of the firm?	😣😖😐🙂😄
Within what price range would you feel comfortable adding this stock?	
What's the maximum percentage of your portfolio you're comfortable investing in this stock?	

What am I expecting? (Circle all that apply)

Falling interest rates	Reduction in debt	Clearly undervalued
Positive capex cycle	Change in business model	Consistent compounder
Demand-supply mismatch	Merger or Acquisition	Dividend play
Positive government policies	Positive management change	Recession resistant play
Sector Tailwind/Seasonal	Accelerated growth	20+ Year Growth Story
Turnaround story	Enhanced product offerings	Technical signal
Inflation Hedge	Improving Financials	Momentum Play

In 2 lines explain why you are buying this stock

Post Trade Thoughts

Stock _______________________   Date _______________________

Price _______________________   Quantity _______________________

THOUGHTS AFTER SELLING	INPUTS
How confident are you in the business model?	😣 😦 😐 😊 😀
How confident are you in the management?	😣 😦 😐 😊 😀
Rank the financial strength of the firm	😣 😦 😐 😊 😀
How comfortable are you with the valuation of the firm?	😣 😦 😐 😊 😀
If you're selling gradually over time, what price range feels comfortable for you to sell the stock within?	
What return have you generated through this investment?	

Why did I sell the stock?

Did the investment thesis play out as planned?

Pre Trade Thoughts

Stock _______________________   Date _______________________

Price _______________________   Quantity _______________________

THOUGHTS BEFORE BUYING	INPUTS
How confident are you in the business model?	😡😟😐🙂😄
How confident are you in the management?	😡😟😐🙂😄
Rank the financial strength of the firm	😡😟😐🙂😄
How comfortable are you with the valuation of the firm?	😡😟😐🙂😄
Within what price range would you feel comfortable adding this stock?	
What's the maximum percentage of your portfolio you're comfortable investing in this stock?	

What am I expecting? (Circle all that apply)

Falling interest rates	Reduction in debt	Clearly undervalued
Positive capex cycle	Change in business model	Consistent compounder
Demand-supply mismatch	Merger or Acquisition	Dividend play
Positive government policies	Positive management change	Recession resistant play
Sector Tailwind/Seasonal	Accelerated growth	20+ Year Growth Story
Turnaround story	Enhanced product offerings	Technical signal
Inflation Hedge	Improving Financials	Momentum Play

In 2 lines explain why you are buying this stock

Post Trade Thoughts

Stock ....   Date ....

Price ....   Quantity ....

THOUGHTS AFTER SELLING	INPUTS
How confident are you in the business model?	☹ ☹ 😐 😊 😀
How confident are you in the management?	☹ ☹ 😐 😊 😀
Rank the financial strength of the firm	☹ ☹ 😐 😊 😀
How comfortable are you with the valuation of the firm?	☹ ☹ 😐 😊 😀
If you're selling gradually over time, what price range feels comfortable for you to sell the stock within?	
What return have you generated through this investment?	

Why did I sell the stock?

Did the investment thesis play out as planned?

Pre Trade Thoughts

Stock ....   Date ....

Price ....   Quantity ....

THOUGHTS BEFORE BUYING	INPUTS
How confident are you in the business model?	😣😟😐🙂😄
How confident are you in the management?	😣😟😐🙂😄
Rank the financial strength of the firm	😣😟😐🙂😄
How comfortable are you with the valuation of the firm?	😣😟😐🙂😄
Within what price range would you feel comfortable adding this stock?	
What's the maximum percentage of your portfolio you're comfortable investing in this stock?	

What am I expecting? (Circle all that apply)

Falling interest rates	Reduction in debt	Clearly undervalued
Positive capex cycle	Change in business model	Consistent compounder
Demand-supply mismatch	Merger or Acquisition	Dividend play
Positive government policies	Positive management change	Recession resistant play
Sector Tailwind/Seasonal	Accelerated growth	20+ Year Growth Story
Turnaround story	Enhanced product offerings	Technical signal
Inflation Hedge	Improving Financials	Momentum Play

In 2 lines explain why you are buying this stock

Post Trade Thoughts

Stock ___________________________   Date ___________________

Price ___________________________   Quantity _______________

THOUGHTS AFTER SELLING	INPUTS
How confident are you in the business model?	☹☹😐🙂😃
How confident are you in the management?	☹☹😐🙂😃
Rank the financial strength of the firm	☹☹😐🙂😃
How comfortable are you with the valuation of the firm?	☹☹😐🙂😃
If you're selling gradually over time, what price range feels comfortable for you to sell the stock within?	
What return have you generated through this investment?	

Why did I sell the stock?

Did the investment thesis play out as planned?

Pre Trade Thoughts

Stock ....   Date ....

Price ....   Quantity ....

THOUGHTS BEFORE BUYING	INPUTS
How confident are you in the business model?	😞😞😐😊😃
How confident are you in the management?	😞😞😐😊😃
Rank the financial strength of the firm	😞😞😐😊😃
How comfortable are you with the valuation of the firm?	😞😞😐😊😃
Within what price range would you feel comfortable adding this stock?	
What's the maximum percentage of your portfolio you're comfortable investing in this stock?	

What am I expecting? (Circle all that apply)

Falling interest rates	Reduction in debt	Clearly undervalued
Positive capex cycle	Change in business model	Consistent compounder
Demand-supply mismatch	Merger or Acquisition	Dividend play
Positive government policies	Positive management change	Recession resistant play
Sector Tailwind/Seasonal	Accelerated growth	20+ Year Growth Story
Turnaround story	Enhanced product offerings	Technical signal
Inflation Hedge	Improving Financials	Momentum Play

In 2 lines explain why you are buying this stock

Post Trade Thoughts

Stock .... Date ....

Price .... Quantity ....

THOUGHTS AFTER SELLING	INPUTS
How confident are you in the business model?	😞 😟 😐 🙂 😀
How confident are you in the management?	😞 😟 😐 🙂 😀
Rank the financial strength of the firm	😞 😟 😐 🙂 😀
How comfortable are you with the valuation of the firm?	😞 😟 😐 🙂 😀
If you're selling gradually over time, what price range feels comfortable for you to sell the stock within?	
What return have you generated through this investment?	

Why did I sell the stock?

Did the investment thesis play out as planned?

Pre Trade Thoughts

Stock ______________________________   Date ______________________________

Price ______________________________   Quantity ______________________________

THOUGHTS BEFORE BUYING	INPUTS
How confident are you in the business model?	😠😣😐🙂😀
How confident are you in the management?	😠😣😐🙂😀
Rank the financial strength of the firm	😠😣😐🙂😀
How comfortable are you with the valuation of the firm?	😠😣😐🙂😀
Within what price range would you feel comfortable adding this stock?	
What's the maximum percentage of your portfolio you're comfortable investing in this stock?	

What am I expecting? (Circle all that apply)

Falling interest rates	Reduction in debt	Clearly undervalued
Positive capex cycle	Change in business model	Consistent compounder
Demand-supply mismatch	Merger or Acquisition	Dividend play
Positive government policies	Positive management change	Recession resistant play
Sector Tailwind/Seasonal	Accelerated growth	20+ Year Growth Story
Turnaround story	Enhanced product offerings	Technical signal
Inflation Hedge	Improving Financials	Momentum Play

In 2 lines explain why you are buying this stock

Post Trade Thoughts

Stock _______________________   Date _______________________

Price _______________________   Quantity _______________________

THOUGHTS AFTER SELLING	INPUTS
How confident are you in the business model?	😫😟😐😊😃
How confident are you in the management?	😫😟😐😊😃
Rank the financial strength of the firm	😫😟😐😊😃
How comfortable are you with the valuation of the firm?	😫😟😐😊😃
If you're selling gradually over time, what price range feels comfortable for you to sell the stock within?	
What return have you generated through this investment?	

Why did I sell the stock?

Did the investment thesis play out as planned?

Pre Trade Thoughts

Stock .... Date ....

Price .... Quantity ....

THOUGHTS BEFORE BUYING	INPUTS
How confident are you in the business model?	😫😟😐🙂😀
How confident are you in the management?	😫😟😐🙂😀
Rank the financial strength of the firm	😫😟😐🙂😀
How comfortable are you with the valuation of the firm?	😫😟😐🙂😀
Within what price range would you feel comfortable adding this stock?	
What's the maximum percentage of your portfolio you're comfortable investing in this stock?	

What am I expecting? (Circle all that apply)

Falling interest rates	Reduction in debt	Clearly undervalued
Positive capex cycle	Change in business model	Consistent compounder
Demand-supply mismatch	Merger or Acquisition	Dividend play
Positive government policies	Positive management change	Recession resistant play
Sector Tailwind/Seasonal	Accelerated growth	20+ Year Growth Story
Turnaround story	Enhanced product offerings	Technical signal
Inflation Hedge	Improving Financials	Momentum Play

In 2 lines explain why you are buying this stock

Post Trade Thoughts

Stock _________________________   Date _________________________

Price _________________________   Quantity _________________________

THOUGHTS AFTER SELLING	INPUTS
How confident are you in the business model?	😟😟😐🙂😀
How confident are you in the management?	😟😟😐🙂😀
Rank the financial strength of the firm	😟😟😐🙂😀
How comfortable are you with the valuation of the firm?	😟😟😐🙂😀
If you're selling gradually over time, what price range feels comfortable for you to sell the stock within?	
What return have you generated through this investment?	

Why did I sell the stock?

Did the investment thesis play out as planned?

Pre Trade Thoughts

Stock .... Date ....

Price .... Quantity ....

THOUGHTS BEFORE BUYING	INPUTS
How confident are you in the business model?	😦 😧 😐 🙂 😀
How confident are you in the management?	😦 😧 😐 🙂 😀
Rank the financial strength of the firm	😦 😧 😐 🙂 😀
How comfortable are you with the valuation of the firm?	😦 😧 😐 🙂 😀
Within what price range would you feel comfortable adding this stock?	
What's the maximum percentage of your portfolio you're comfortable investing in this stock?	

What am I expecting? (Circle all that apply)

Falling interest rates	Reduction in debt	Clearly undervalued
Positive capex cycle	Change in business model	Consistent compounder
Demand-supply mismatch	Merger or Acquisition	Dividend play
Positive government policies	Positive management change	Recession resistant play
Sector Tailwind/Seasonal	Accelerated growth	20+ Year Growth Story
Turnaround story	Enhanced product offerings	Technical signal
Inflation Hedge	Improving Financials	Momentum Play

In 2 lines explain why you are buying this stock

Post Trade Thoughts

Stock ....   Date ....

Price ....   Quantity ....

THOUGHTS AFTER SELLING	INPUTS
How confident are you in the business model?	😠😟😐😊😀
How confident are you in the management?	😠😟😐😊😀
Rank the financial strength of the firm	😠😟😐😊😀
How comfortable are you with the valuation of the firm?	😠😟😐😊😀
If you're selling gradually over time, what price range feels comfortable for you to sell the stock within?	
What return have you generated through this investment?	

Why did I sell the stock?

Did the investment thesis play out as planned?

Pre Trade Thoughts

Stock _______________________   Date _______________________

Price _______________________   Quantity _______________________

THOUGHTS BEFORE BUYING	INPUTS
How confident are you in the business model?	😩😟😐😊😃
How confident are you in the management?	😩😟😐😊😃
Rank the financial strength of the firm	😩😟😐😊😃
How comfortable are you with the valuation of the firm?	😩😟😐😊😃
Within what price range would you feel comfortable adding this stock?	
What's the maximum percentage of your portfolio you're comfortable investing in this stock?	

What am I expecting? (Circle all that apply)

Falling interest rates	Reduction in debt	Clearly undervalued
Positive capex cycle	Change in business model	Consistent compounder
Demand-supply mismatch	Merger or Acquisition	Dividend play
Positive government policies	Positive management change	Recession resistant play
Sector Tailwind/Seasonal	Accelerated growth	20+ Year Growth Story
Turnaround story	Enhanced product offerings	Technical signal
Inflation Hedge	Improving Financials	Momentum Play

In 2 lines explain why you are buying this stock

Post Trade Thoughts

Stock ___________________________   Date ___________________________

Price ___________________________   Quantity ___________________________

THOUGHTS AFTER SELLING	INPUTS
How confident are you in the business model?	☹ ☹ 😐 😊 😀
How confident are you in the management?	☹ ☹ 😐 😊 😀
Rank the financial strength of the firm	☹ ☹ 😐 😊 😀
How comfortable are you with the valuation of the firm?	☹ ☹ 😐 😊 😀
If you're selling gradually over time, what price range feels comfortable for you to sell the stock within?	
What return have you generated through this investment?	

Why did I sell the stock?

Did the investment thesis play out as planned?

Pre Trade Thoughts

Stock ___________________________   Date ___________________________

Price ___________________________   Quantity ___________________________

THOUGHTS BEFORE BUYING	INPUTS
How confident are you in the business model?	😦😦😐😊😄
How confident are you in the management?	😦😦😐😊😄
Rank the financial strength of the firm	😦😦😐😊😄
How comfortable are you with the valuation of the firm?	😦😦😐😊😄
Within what price range would you feel comfortable adding this stock?	
What's the maximum percentage of your portfolio you're comfortable investing in this stock?	

What am I expecting? (Circle all that apply)

Falling interest rates	Reduction in debt	Clearly undervalued
Positive capex cycle	Change in business model	Consistent compounder
Demand-supply mismatch	Merger or Acquisition	Dividend play
Positive government policies	Positive management change	Recession resistant play
Sector Tailwind/Seasonal	Accelerated growth	20+ Year Growth Story
Turnaround story	Enhanced product offerings	Technical signal
Inflation Hedge	Improving Financials	Momentum Play

In 2 lines explain why you are buying this stock

Post Trade Thoughts

Stock _______________________   Date _______________________

Price _______________________   Quantity _______________________

THOUGHTS AFTER SELLING	INPUTS
How confident are you in the business model?	😫😣😐🙂😀
How confident are you in the management?	😫😣😐🙂😀
Rank the financial strength of the firm	😫😣😐🙂😀
How comfortable are you with the valuation of the firm?	😫😣😐🙂😀
If you're selling gradually over time, what price range feels comfortable for you to sell the stock within?	
What return have you generated through this investment?	

Why did I sell the stock?

Did the investment thesis play out as planned?

Pre Trade Thoughts

Stock .... Date ....

Price .... Quantity ....

THOUGHTS BEFORE BUYING	INPUTS
How confident are you in the business model?	😦 😦 😐 😊 😀
How confident are you in the management?	😦 😦 😐 😊 😀
Rank the financial strength of the firm	😦 😦 😐 😊 😀
How comfortable are you with the valuation of the firm?	😦 😦 😐 😊 😀
Within what price range would you feel comfortable adding this stock?	
What's the maximum percentage of your portfolio you're comfortable investing in this stock?	

What am I expecting? (Circle all that apply)

Falling interest rates	Reduction in debt	Clearly undervalued
Positive capex cycle	Change in business model	Consistent compounder
Demand-supply mismatch	Merger or Acquisition	Dividend play
Positive government policies	Positive management change	Recession resistant play
Sector Tailwind/Seasonal	Accelerated growth	20+ Year Growth Story
Turnaround story	Enhanced product offerings	Technical signal
Inflation Hedge	Improving Financials	Momentum Play

In 2 lines explain why you are buying this stock

Post Trade Thoughts

Stock ________________________   Date ________________________

Price ________________________   Quantity ________________________

THOUGHTS AFTER SELLING	INPUTS
How confident are you in the business model?	😟 😦 😐 🙂 😄
How confident are you in the management?	😟 😦 😐 🙂 😄
Rank the financial strength of the firm	😟 😦 😐 🙂 😄
How comfortable are you with the valuation of the firm?	😟 😦 😐 🙂 😄
If you're selling gradually over time, what price range feels comfortable for you to sell the stock within?	
What return have you generated through this investment?	

Why did I sell the stock?

Did the investment thesis play out as planned?

Pre Trade Thoughts

Stock ______________________   Date ______________________

Price ______________________   Quantity ______________________

THOUGHTS BEFORE BUYING	INPUTS
How confident are you in the business model?	� � 😐 🙂 😄
How confident are you in the management?	� � 😐 🙂 😄
Rank the financial strength of the firm	� � 😐 🙂 😄
How comfortable are you with the valuation of the firm?	� � 😐 🙂 😄
Within what price range would you feel comfortable adding this stock?	
What's the maximum percentage of your portfolio you're comfortable investing in this stock?	

What am I expecting? (Circle all that apply)

Falling interest rates	Reduction in debt	Clearly undervalued
Positive capex cycle	Change in business model	Consistent compounder
Demand-supply mismatch	Merger or Acquisition	Dividend play
Positive government policies	Positive management change	Recession resistant play
Sector Tailwind/Seasonal	Accelerated growth	20+ Year Growth Story
Turnaround story	Enhanced product offerings	Technical signal
Inflation Hedge	Improving Financials	Momentum Play

In 2 lines explain why you are buying this stock

Post Trade Thoughts

Stock _______________________   Date _______________________

Price _______________________   Quantity _______________________

THOUGHTS AFTER SELLING	INPUTS
How confident are you in the business model?	😣😟😐😊😁
How confident are you in the management?	😣😟😐😊😁
Rank the financial strength of the firm	😣😟😐😊😁
How comfortable are you with the valuation of the firm?	😣😟😐😊😁
If you're selling gradually over time, what price range feels comfortable for you to sell the stock within?	
What return have you generated through this investment?	

Why did I sell the stock?

Did the investment thesis play out as planned?

Pre Trade Thoughts

Stock _________________________   Date _________________________

Price _________________________   Quantity _________________________

THOUGHTS BEFORE BUYING	INPUTS
How confident are you in the business model?	😣😦😐😊😃
How confident are you in the management?	😣😦😐😊😃
Rank the financial strength of the firm	😣😦😐😊😃
How comfortable are you with the valuation of the firm?	😣😦😐😊😃
Within what price range would you feel comfortable adding this stock?	
What's the maximum percentage of your portfolio you're comfortable investing in this stock?	

What am I expecting? (Circle all that apply)

Falling interest rates	Reduction in debt	Clearly undervalued
Positive capex cycle	Change in business model	Consistent compounder
Demand-supply mismatch	Merger or Acquisition	Dividend play
Positive government policies	Positive management change	Recession resistant play
Sector Tailwind/Seasonal	Accelerated growth	20+ Year Growth Story
Turnaround story	Enhanced product offerings	Technical signal
Inflation Hedge	Improving Financials	Momentum Play

In 2 lines explain why you are buying this stock

Post Trade Thoughts

Stock _____________________   Date _____________________

Price _____________________   Quantity _____________________

THOUGHTS AFTER SELLING	INPUTS
How confident are you in the business model?	😦 😦 😐 😊 😃
How confident are you in the management?	😦 😦 😐 😊 😃
Rank the financial strength of the firm	😦 😦 😐 😊 😃
How comfortable are you with the valuation of the firm?	😦 😦 😐 😊 😃
If you're selling gradually over time, what price range feels comfortable for you to sell the stock within?	
What return have you generated through this investment?	

Why did I sell the stock?

Did the investment thesis play out as planned?

Pre Trade Thoughts

Stock ....   Date ....

Price ....   Quantity ....

THOUGHTS BEFORE BUYING	INPUTS
How confident are you in the business model?	☹️ 😕 😐 🙂 😄
How confident are you in the management?	☹️ 😕 😐 🙂 😄
Rank the financial strength of the firm	☹️ 😕 😐 🙂 😄
How comfortable are you with the valuation of the firm?	☹️ 😕 😐 🙂 😄
Within what price range would you feel comfortable adding this stock?	
What's the maximum percentage of your portfolio you're comfortable investing in this stock?	

What am I expecting? (Circle all that apply)

Falling interest rates	Reduction in debt	Clearly undervalued
Positive capex cycle	Change in business model	Consistent compounder
Demand-supply mismatch	Merger or Acquisition	Dividend play
Positive government policies	Positive management change	Recession resistant play
Sector Tailwind/Seasonal	Accelerated growth	20+ Year Growth Story
Turnaround story	Enhanced product offerings	Technical signal
Inflation Hedge	Improving Financials	Momentum Play

In 2 lines explain why you are buying this stock

Post Trade Thoughts

Stock ....   Date ....

Price ....   Quantity ....

THOUGHTS AFTER SELLING	INPUTS
How confident are you in the business model?	😧😠😐😊😃
How confident are you in the management?	😧😠😐😊😃
Rank the financial strength of the firm	😧😠😐😊😃
How comfortable are you with the valuation of the firm?	😧😠😐😊😃
If you're selling gradually over time, what price range feels comfortable for you to sell the stock within?	
What return have you generated through this investment?	

Why did I sell the stock?

Did the investment thesis play out as planned?

Pre Trade Thoughts

Stock _______________________   Date _______________________

Price _______________________   Quantity _______________________

THOUGHTS BEFORE BUYING	INPUTS
How confident are you in the business model?	😠😟😐🙂😄
How confident are you in the management?	😠😟😐🙂😄
Rank the financial strength of the firm	😠😟😐🙂😄
How comfortable are you with the valuation of the firm?	😠😟😐🙂😄
Within what price range would you feel comfortable adding this stock?	
What's the maximum percentage of your portfolio you're comfortable investing in this stock?	

What am I expecting? (Circle all that apply)

Falling interest rates	Reduction in debt	Clearly undervalued
Positive capex cycle	Change in business model	Consistent compounder
Demand-supply mismatch	Merger or Acquisition	Dividend play
Positive government policies	Positive management change	Recession resistant play
Sector Tailwind/Seasonal	Accelerated growth	20+ Year Growth Story
Turnaround story	Enhanced product offerings	Technical signal
Inflation Hedge	Improving Financials	Momentum Play

In 2 lines explain why you are buying this stock

Post Trade Thoughts

Stock __________________________   Date __________________________

Price __________________________   Quantity __________________________

THOUGHTS AFTER SELLING	INPUTS
How confident are you in the business model?	☹ ☹ 😐 🙂 😀
How confident are you in the management?	☹ ☹ 😐 🙂 😀
Rank the financial strength of the firm	☹ ☹ 😐 🙂 😀
How comfortable are you with the valuation of the firm?	☹ ☹ 😐 🙂 😀
If you're selling gradually over time, what price range feels comfortable for you to sell the stock within?	
What return have you generated through this investment?	

Why did I sell the stock?

Did the investment thesis play out as planned?

Quarterly check in

DATE _______________

STOCKS THAT INTRIGUE ME

○ _______________

○ _______________

○ _______________

HOW AM I FEELING?

ANY SECTOR OR THEME WORTH HIGHLIGHTING?

____

THOUGHTS?

____

____

____

____

____

____

____

____

____

____

____

Quarterly check in

DATE _______________

STOCKS THAT INTRIGUE ME

○ _______________

○ _______________

○ _______________

HOW AM I FEELING?

THOUGHTS?

ANY SECTOR OR THEME WORTH HIGHLIGHTING?

Quarterly check in DATE ________________

STOCKS THAT INTRIGUE ME
- ○ _______________________
- ○ _______________________
- ○ _______________________

HOW AM I FEELING?

ANY SECTOR OR THEME WORTH HIGHLIGHTING?

THOUGHTS?

Quarterly check in

DATE _______________

STOCKS THAT INTRIGUE ME

○ _______________

○ _______________

○ _______________

ANY SECTOR OR THEME W0RTH HIGHLIGHTING?

HOW AM I FEELING?

THOUGHTS?

Thoughts

DATE ____________________

Thoughts

DATE _______________

Thoughts

DATE ___________________

Thoughts

DATE _______________

Thoughts

DATE _______________

DATE _______________

Thoughts

DATE ______________

Thoughts

DATE _______________

Thoughts

DATE _______________

Thoughts

DATE _______________

Thoughts

DATE _______________

DATE ______________

Thoughts

DATE ___________________